MYSTERIES & MARVELS
OF THE
REPTILE
WORLD

Ian Spellerberg and Marit McKerchar

Designed by Linda Sandey

Illustrated by David Quinn,
Craig Austin (Garden Studios),
Ian Jackson and Sam Thompson

Cartoons by John Shackell

The Arboreal Pit Viper's strong prehensile tail helps it climb trees.

The Red Bellied Turtle forages for food at the edge of the lake.

Contents

4   Warming up and keeping cool
6   Super senses
8   Catching food
10   Fangs and poisons
12   Escape and defence
14   The art of bluff
16   Frills and decorations
18   Courtship
20   Eggs and nurseries
22   On the move
24   Taking to the water
26   A place to live
28   Curious events
30   Record breakers
32   Were they true or false?
Index

Jackson's Chameleon has three horns which may help in defence against predators, such as birds.

By using its large food pouch, the Monitor Lizard often swallows prey, such as a Palm Squirrel, whole.

The Galapagos Tortoise lives on the Island's lowlands and wanders along paths, which have been beaten by generations, to the highlands for food and water.

When disturbed by a predator, the small Royal Ball Python of West Africa throws itself into a ball-like coil, its head in the middle.

About this book

This book is an exciting introduction to the world of reptiles. By looking at some of the more unusual, extraordinary and unexplained aspects of reptile life – how they move, track down and kill their food, care for their young – it provides a stimulating starting point for the study of this fascinating group of creatures.

Reptiles are "cold-blooded" and have to rely on their surroundings to keep their bodies at the right temperature, using various ways to warm up or cool down. They are unlike mammals which use food to heat themselves internally. All reptiles have scales which protect them from losing moisture through the skin and they all, including sea snakes, breathe air. Most lay eggs and these are always laid on land.

Reptiles are often feared as dangerous, slimy creatures. This book introduces some very beautiful ones and will lead to an understanding of the variety and complexity of reptiles.

The Common Iguana is often found in tree tops up to 20m above the ground. If disturbed, it will drop to the ground from heights of up to 6m.

The young crocodile calls to its mother with piercing squeaks as it breaks out of its egg shell.

The striking eye-like patterns on the male Ocellated Gecko's back confuses its enemies.

TRUE or FALSE?

Look out for these questions and try to guess if they are true or false. The answers are on p.32.

Warming up and keeping cool

Reptiles are 'cold-blooded' and they have to rely on their surroundings to keep their bodies at a temperature of 30-35°C. 'Warm-blooded' animals keep their bodies warm by using food as fuel for their internal 'burners'. This difference explains why warm-blooded animals need fairly regular meals while reptiles, such as snakes, can survive on one very large meal every few weeks or even once a year. The behaviour of many reptiles is the result of this need to stay at a steady temperature.

Winter store

Some lizards hibernate in winter, going into a long, cool sleep. They do not eat during this time but use fat stored in their bodies. The large, stumpy tail of the South Australian Shingleback lizard is thought to be a winter store of fat.

Shingleback Lizard

Its tail, which looks very much like its head, may also confuse enemies as they may attack the wrong end.

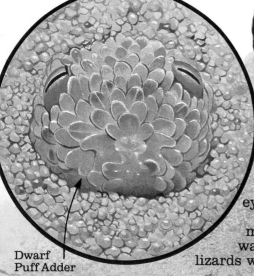

Dwarf Puff Adder

◀Cool hiding place

The Dwarf Puff Adder hides its body from the hot sun by burying itself in the desert sand. Only its eyes show above the surface. As well as keeping cool, the snake lies motionless for hours and even days, waiting to ambush small rodents and lizards which come close enough to provide a meal.

Dancing Lizards▼

The Fringe-Toed Lizard of Southwestern Africa 'dances' to keep cool. It lifts each foot in turn off the hot desert sand and sometimes raises all four feet at once, resting on its stomach. Like many other lizards, this lizard buries itself when the sun is at its hottest. Flaps over its ears and nose keep out the sand when it is underground.

The long, fringed toes help the lizard to run very fast over soft, loose sand in the Namib Desert – one of the hottest places on earth.

Fringe-Toed Lizards

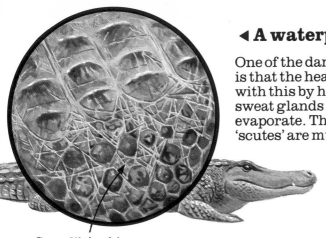

Crocodile's skin

◀ A waterproof skin

One of the dangers of warming up by basking in the sun is that the heat can also dry out the body. Reptiles cope with this by having almost watertight skins, with no sweat glands through which water in their bodies could evaporate. The scales of crocodiles and alligators, called 'scutes' are much larger on their backs, making the skin more waterproof. The scales underneath, shaded from the sun are smaller and more flexible.

▼ In and out of the sun

Each morning, before starting the days hunting for insects, spiders, worms and birds' eggs, the Jewelled Lizard lies in the sun to raise its temperature to 30-35°C. When warm, it is very active but soon becomes too hot. It then runs into the shade to cool down. For the rest of the day, it shuttles in and out of the sun to keep its body at the right temperature.

A Jewelled Lizard using the shade. Growing up to 75cm long, it can run very fast over sand and rocks.

TRUE or FALSE?

Skinks have anti-freeze in their blood.

Cool character ▲

The Tuatara is a unique reptile, being able to survive on the small cold islands off New Zealand. Most reptiles live in warm areas as it is easier for them to cool down by keeping out of the sun than to warm up if the air is cold. The Tuatara is active at body temperatures lower than those of any other reptile and keeps its body at about 12°C.

As its body is so cool, this lizard is very slow. When moving, it breathes about once every seven seconds but this slows down to about once an hour when it is still. It also grows slowly taking 20 years to reach a length of about 60cm.

Tuataras spend most of the day in their burrows but often lie in the sun in the morning and evening. They come out at night to hunt for insects and spiders but also eat worms and snails.

5

Super senses

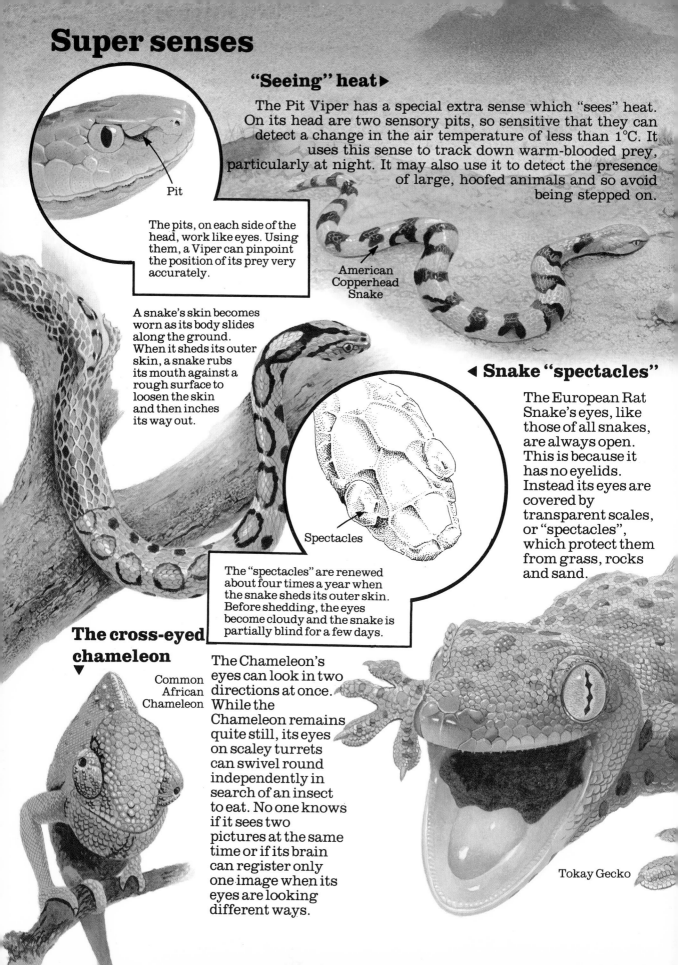

"Seeing" heat ▶

The Pit Viper has a special extra sense which "sees" heat. On its head are two sensory pits, so sensitive that they can detect a change in the air temperature of less than 1°C. It uses this sense to track down warm-blooded prey, particularly at night. It may also use it to detect the presence of large, hoofed animals and so avoid being stepped on.

Pit

The pits, on each side of the head, work like eyes. Using them, a Viper can pinpoint the position of its prey very accurately.

American Copperhead Snake

A snake's skin becomes worn as its body slides along the ground. When it sheds its outer skin, a snake rubs its mouth against a rough surface to loosen the skin and then inches its way out.

◀ Snake "spectacles"

The European Rat Snake's eyes, like those of all snakes, are always open. This is because it has no eyelids. Instead its eyes are covered by transparent scales, or "spectacles", which protect them from grass, rocks and sand.

Spectacles

The "spectacles" are renewed about four times a year when the snake sheds its outer skin. Before shedding, the eyes become cloudy and the snake is partially blind for a few days.

The cross-eyed chameleon
▼

Common African Chameleon

The Chameleon's eyes can look in two directions at once. While the Chameleon remains quite still, its eyes on scaley turrets can swivel round independently in search of an insect to eat. No one knows if it sees two pictures at the same time or if its brain can register only one image when its eyes are looking different ways.

Tokay Gecko

Kangaroo Rat

It follows the Rat down the dark tunnel of its burrow.

This Pit Viper, an American Copperhead, detects the heat given off by the body of a Kangaroo Rat about 50cm away.

When the Viper reaches the Rat, its pits detect the place and distance of its prey. The snake then strikes and kills with its poisonous fangs.

Jacobson's organ

In the mouths of snakes and lizards are two openings which lead to the Jacobson's organ. This extra sense organ detects and identifies the smell of a meal or a mate.

"Tasting" the air ▼

The forked tongues of snakes and lizards are not poisonous, as is often believed. They are harmless and are used to "taste" the air. The flicking tongue picks up smell particles from the air and ground and delivers them to the Jacobson's organ in the roof of the mouth.

The Nile Monitor uses its tongue to find its prey of small mammals, snakes and lizards. Growing to over 2m long, it also steals eggs from crocodiles' nests.

◄ Wide eyes

The common Tropical Gecko hunts at night and has huge eyes with very large pupils in order to see as much as possible in the dark. In daylight, the pupils close up, leaving four tiny pinholes, so only a small amount of light can enter the eyes. It uses its long tongue to clean its eyes which have no eyelids.

The Gecko does not see four pictures out of the pinholes but one sharp image.

TRUE or FALSE?

The Cobra dances to the music of the snake charmer's pipe.

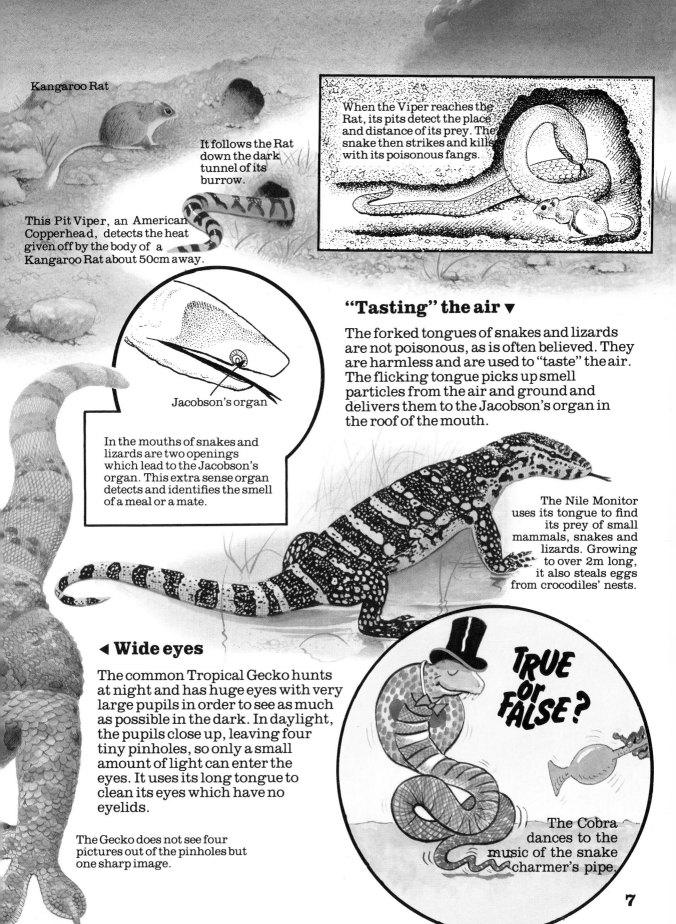

7

Catching food

Catapult tongue ▼

During the day, the Chameleon moves slowly along the branches of trees in the forest hunting for insects and spiders to eat.

When near enough to its prey, it wraps its tail firmly round a twig, watching its target. Suddenly it shoots out its tongue, which stretches up to the length of its own body, with great accuracy. Then its tongue springs back into its mouth, bringing in the meal. The whole action takes less than a second.

Graceful Chameleon

The round end of the tongue acts like a suction pad and sticks to the prey. Back inside the mouth, the tongue is short and fat. It is like a sleeve of muscle round a long "launching bone" on the Chameleon's lower jaw.

Sticky suction pad

Launching bone

Causing a current

The Matamata Turtle lurks in the muddy rivers of Brazil. When small fish swim close, it opens its jaws so quickly that the fish are swept into its mouth by the current of water this makes.

Using its long neck, the turtle can hold its nostrils out of the water and breathe without moving and scaring the fish. Algae growing on the bumpy 40cm shell helps to camouflage the turtle.

Long tassels of skin look like weed and tempt passing fish to swim close.

False worm ▼

The Alligator Snapping Turtle's colours exactly match the muddy waters of the rivers in North America where it lives. It lies on the river bed with its mouth wide open, completely still except for its bright tongue which it wiggles to look like a worm. Hungry fish dart into its mouth after the "worm", the turtle snaps its jaws shut and swallows the fish. This turtle gets its name from its strong alligator-like tail and powerful jaws.

Weighing up to 100kg and 75cm long, this is the largest of the American fresh-water turtles.

Alligator Snapping Turtle.

Super swallowers ▼

The Boa Constrictor strikes its prey swiftly with its long, sharp teeth. The teeth slope backwards into the mouth so the more a victim struggles, the more firmly it is wedged on to them. The 2m Rainbow Boa suffocates its prey by squeezing it and then swallows it whole. A Boa, like all snakes, can swallow birds and other animals thicker than its own body because of its amazing jaw — the two halves move right apart at the hinge and are joined only by muscle.

Egg eater

The African egg-eating snake lives in trees where it searches birds' nests hoping to find a meal of eggs. It often swallows eggs which are more than twice the width of its own body.

The snake stretches its elasticated jaws wide apart to fit round the egg, which it grips with its blunt teeth.

In its throat 30 special "teeth", which are extensions of the snake's spine, break the shell as the egg is swallowed. The egg white and yolk flow into the snake's stomach but the shell remains outside and is regurgitated.

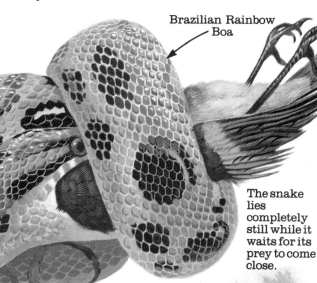

Brazilian Rainbow Boa

The snake lies completely still while it waits for its prey to come close.

A snorkel-like windpipe allows the snake to breathe while it swallows a large meal. A 7.5m Python was seen to eat a pig weighing about 54kg and later it swallowed a 47kg goat.

Living larder ▶

The Australian Blind Snake lives in its larder — a termites' nest, where it feeds on its termite hosts. Surprisingly, the soldier termites do not often attack the snake. This may be because the snake smells like the termites and so goes unnoticed in the dark tunnels of the mound.

Compass Termites get their name from their mounds which they build in a north-south direction. The tower-like mounds are 3m high by 21m wide, but only 8-10cm thick. Their orientation helps reduce heat in summer but makes the most of winter sun.

The Blind Snake, about 40cm long, inside the termites' nest.

The snake's shiny skin acts like a smooth armour protecting it against bites from the termites' powerful jaws.

Fangs and poisons

Poisonous lizards

Of the 3,000 different kinds of lizards only two, the Gila Monster of North America and the Mexican Beaded Lizard, are poisonous. The Gila Monster does not have fangs to inject its poison. Instead, the venom flows from glands in its lower jaw on to grooves in its bottom teeth. When the Gila Monster bites its victim, venom washes around the teeth and is chewed into the wound. The potent venom acts on the victim's nerves and muscles causing internal bleeding and paralysis.

This "Monster" is only just over ½m long and weighs about 1½kg.

Gila Monster

Venomous vipers

The Viper's poison injecting fangs are so long that, when they are not being used, they hinge back against the roof of its mouth.

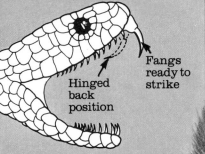

Hinged back position

Fangs ready to strike

The Viper's venom kills its prey by causing its blood to clot. This venom has been used in medicine to help cure blood diseases, such as haemophilia.

The Mongoose is one of the few animals which dares to confront a Cobra. It jumps close, before the Cobra strikes, and grabs the snake's head and jaw.

The Mongoose grips tightly with its teeth and can often win fights with small Cobras which have little chance of injecting their venom.

Spitting Cobra

The venom is squeezed out through holes at the tip of the fangs. It can spit about six times before the venom supply runs out, but this is replaced within a day.

The 2m long Spitting Cobra is found in many parts of Africa.

◄ The venom pistol

The Spitting Cobra squirts a fine stream of venom at its enemy's face, aiming for its eyes. The venom does not kill but it is painful and can make the victim blind. The venom can reach animals up to 3m away but the Cobra's shot is only accurate up to 2m. Using this "weapon" the Cobra can "warn off" its enemy from a safe distance.

King Cobra

Deadly babies

The long fangs of the Fer-de-Lance delivers very deadly venom. The young snakes are born alive in litters of 60-80 babies. Each baby is born complete with fangs and venom, making it dangerous from the start of life. They grow up to nearly 2m long.

The Fer-de-Lance was given its name because of its lance-shaped head and body. It lives in South America and the West Indies, where it is greatly feared because its search for rats and mice has brought it close to human homes.

Head of Fer-de-Lance

◄ The hooded cobra

The King Cobra is the largest poisonous snake, growing up to 5½m. Its tubular fangs stab directly into the victim when it strikes. They are connected to a venom gland which pumps poison through the fangs into the victim. When disturbed, the Cobra raises its body into the strike position, its neck stretched into a threatening hood. Its venom is lethal to most animals, and its fangs deliver more venom than any other snake — one bite can kill an elephant in four hours.

African Boomslang — about 1m long.

Boomslangs have the most deadly poison of any rear-fanged snake, but they rarely bite people as they are shy, hiding away in the trees.

A back-fanged killer ►

Some snakes, such as the Boomslang, have fangs at the back of their mouths rather than at the front.

Chameleon

The short, fragile fangs are set well back in the upper jaw.

When the Boomslang attacks its prey it needs to hold on with its mouth and chew the victim's flesh in order to inject a large dose of venom. This way of poisoning is not as efficient as the speedy strike of front-fanged snakes, but the Boomslang's venom, when injected, is just as deadly.

TRUE or FALSE?

Snakes have been used as weapons of war.

Escape and defence

If cornered by an enemy, this Bearded lizard makes a threatening display. It stretches out the spiny pouch round its throat, making its head look twice its normal size. It expands its body, opens its mouth to show the bright colours inside and hisses, but it rarely bites.

A two-legged escape

The Frilled Lizard of Australia escapes from predators by running away on its hind legs. This is a mystery because it travels faster on all fours. It may be that, as running makes it very hot, it can keep cooler by holding its body upright in the air, above the hot ground.

Frilled Lizard

The lizard, which is over 60cm long, uses its long tail to balance when running fast on two legs.

A shell fortress ▶

The tortoise carries its shell fortress on its back. The shell is made of horny plates, strengthened underneath by bone so that the tortoise's body is enclosed in a box which can resist almost any attack. It can withdraw its head and legs into this box when danger threatens. Under its stomach is another plate of shell, called the plastron, which in some tortoises hinges in the middle. The Box Tortoise can draw up each end of this plate tightly against the top shell, called the carapace.

Radiated Tortoise of Madagascar

This defence is so effective that tortoises and turtles have survived, almost unchanged, for over 200 million years. Not all of them can withdraw into their shells – the Big-Headed Turtle's head, as its name suggests, can not be withdrawn, and the Snake-Necked Turtle bends its neck sideways, along its shell, to tuck it out of sight.

Stinkpot

The tiny, 10cm Stinkpot is North America's smallest water turtle. As well as its shell, it has a second line of defence against predators, such as crows. When disturbed it gives off a terrible smell from special musk glands. This turtle can climb well and the female usually lays her eggs in nests dug on land.

Musk Turtles spend most of their time in pools and sluggish streams. They feed on water insects, tadpoles, snails and fish and often also take fishermen's bait from the end of lines.

◄ Quick change artist

The Chameleon can change the colour and pattern of its skin in order to improve its camouflage in trees where it hunts for insects and is preyed on by snakes. It does this by means of special yellow, black and reflecting white colour cells in its skin. Colour changes are probably controlled by the Chameleon's nervous system which is triggered by light changes as well as by its emotions, such as fear.

The colour cells change in size which varies the concentrations of different colours so a new colour is produced.

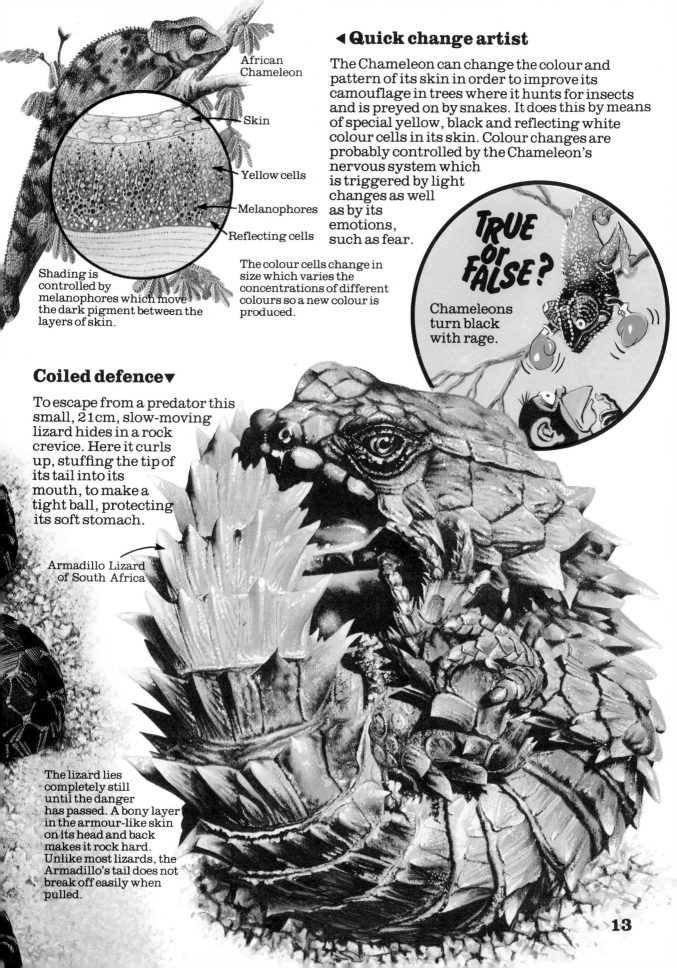

African Chameleon

Skin

Yellow cells

Melanophores

Reflecting cells

Shading is controlled by melanophores which move the dark pigment between the layers of skin.

TRUE or FALSE?

Chameleons turn black with rage.

Coiled defence▼

To escape from a predator this small, 21cm, slow-moving lizard hides in a rock crevice. Here it curls up, stuffing the tip of its tail into its mouth, to make a tight ball, protecting its soft stomach.

Armadillo Lizard of South Africa

The lizard lies completely still until the danger has passed. A bony layer in the armour-like skin on its head and back makes it rock hard. Unlike most lizards, the Armadillo's tail does not break off easily when pulled.

13

The art of bluff

Many reptiles defend themselves by deceiving their enemy in some unusual and curious ways.

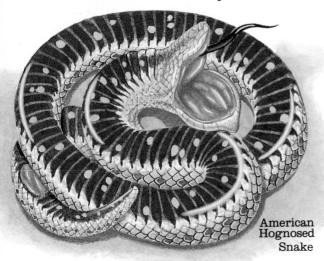

American Hognosed Snake

The inside of the snake's mouth looks like rotting meat and the snake gives off a terrible smell which helps to convince its enemy that it is dead.

◀ Instant death

The Hognosed Snake imitates a Rattlesnake when it meets an enemy. It raises its head and rubs its tail against the side of its body to make a rattling sound. If this does not frighten off the enemy, the snake rolls on to its back and pretends to be dead, lying completely still with its mouth open. Surprisingly, a mammal or bird is usually taken in by this sham, although it saw that the snake was alive only a moment before. Most of them will not eat the flesh of long-dead animals as its tastes unpleasant and could be poisonous.

Snake look-alikes

The Milk Snake protects itself from attack by looking very like the poisonous Coral Snake. The brightly coloured bands on the Coral Snake's body alerts mammals of its poisonous nature. By copying this pattern, the Milk Snake is also thought to be poisonous even though it is quite harmless.

Coral Snake

Milk Snake

The model for the mimic is one of the less poisonous of the many Coral Snakes. Because mammals survive encounters with them, they remember and learn to avoid them in future. The Milk Snake can be told apart from the Coral Snake, as in the rhyme:

Red and black, friend of Jack,
Red and yellow, kill a fellow.

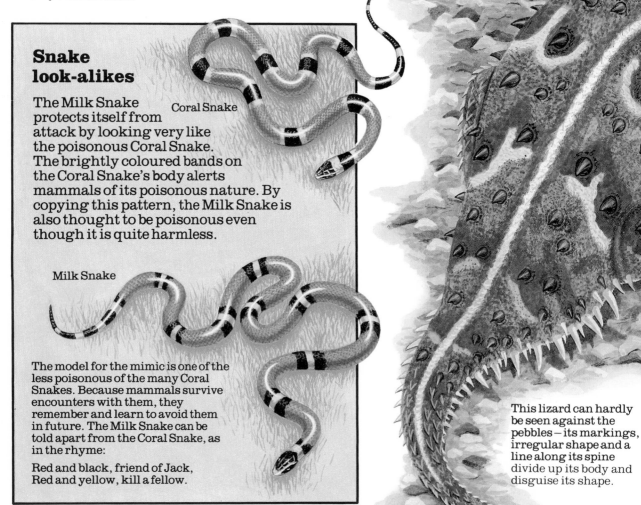

This lizard can hardly be seen against the pebbles – its markings, irregular shape and a line along its spine divide up its body and disguise its shape.

TRUE or FALSE?

Crocodiles pretend to be logs to escape from enemies.

Badger

A sad tail ▶

When grabbed by a predator, a skink's tail breaks off without harming its body. The detached tail goes on wriggling for several minutes, attracting the predator's attention and giving the little lizard time to escape to safety. The bright blue of a young skink's tail would seem to make it an obvious target, but by deliberately drawing an enemy's attention away from its body, the lizard can survive an attack. As the skink grows older, its tail becomes a duller blue.

Horned Toad – a lizard with a toad-like face.

Most lizards' tails can break off. They have a special crack in each of the tail bones, with muscles each side which separate easily. New tails grow again within a couple of seasons, but these are usually shorter than the first tail.

The blood squirter

The Horned Toad startles its enemies by squirting blood from its eyes. No one knows why the lizard does this. The blood spray may irritate its enemy's eyes, or it could fool the enemy into thinking that the lizard has been wounded. Some scientists think that the blood squirt is caused by parasites living in its eyes, and that it has nothing to do with defence. The blood comes from a special eyelid which swells up, and the little lizard — it only grows up to 13cm — can squirt blood up to 1m away.

Sudanese skink

Scars on the gentle 60cm Boa's tail are proof of attacks it has survived by using this clever bluff.

Rubber Boa of Mexico and southwestern U.S.A.

Two-faced snake ▶

When the Rubber Boa is disturbed by an enemy, it coils into a tight ball and hides its head under its body. It raises instead its blunt head-like tail and waves it aggressively at its enemy. If the enemy attacks, it will go for what it thinks is the snake's head, while the real head remains safely hidden.

15

Frills and decorations

Disappearing act ▶

The Leaf-Tailed Gecko of Madagascar is almost impossible to spot, even when seen close to, against the bark of trees where it lives. Its unusual tail, dappled colours and the fringe of scales along its sides and legs give it perfect camouflage. It can curl its tail round to hold on to branches and its huge eyes are useful when hunting at night.

Leaf-Tailed Gecko

Some scientists think that the scaly border acts as a kind of parachute when the gecko jumps from a tree.

Frilled bravado

The Frilled Lizard startles its attackers with an amazing umbrella-like frill. The lizard uses this display only as a last resort. Normally it first sprints away, running on its hind legs with the frill folded round its shoulders. If cornered, the lizard turns to face the enemy with its mouth open, the frill stretched out, its body swaying from side to side. If the enemy is not scared off by this, the lizard steps forward, hissing loudly. Such display is enough to deter most predators, although the lizard is quite harmless.

This lizard is Australia's largest 'dragon' and grows up to about 80 cm long.

Frilled Lizard of Australia

The frill is also thought to cool the lizard as it contains many blood vessels.

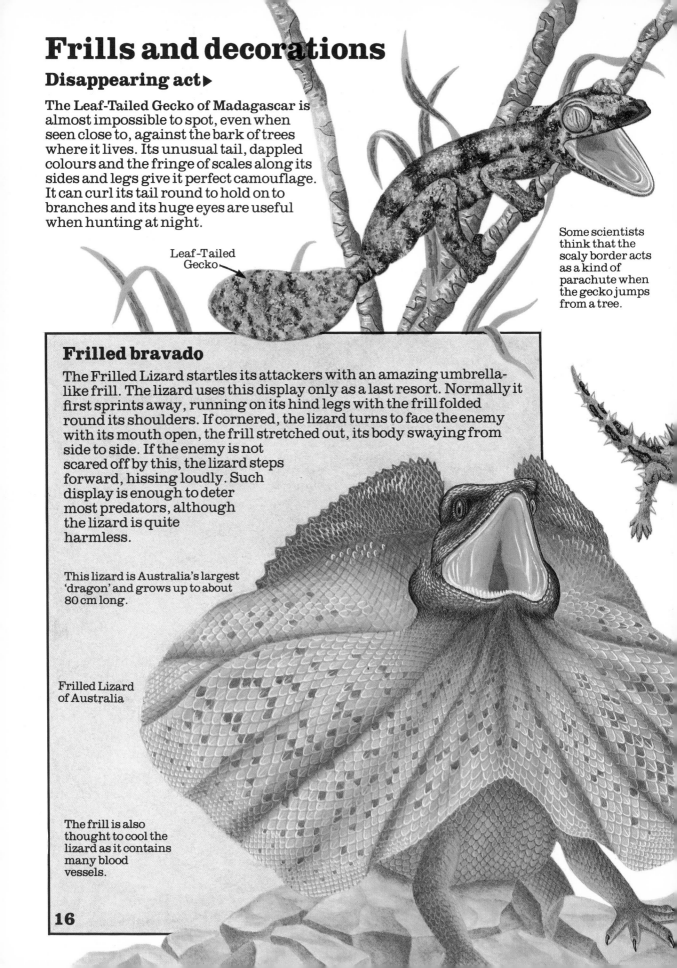

Threatening throat ▶

The male Anole defends his territory against other males by extending his brilliant throat sac. A smaller lizard will retreat immediately but anoles of the same size may display to each other for several hours.

The two males sidle round each other with their bodies puffed up. Then one, followed by the other raises his body off the ground, stretches his throat sac and wags his tail up and down. After a few minutes, they both drop down before starting again. Usually they rarely fight and eventually lose interest in each other and walk away.

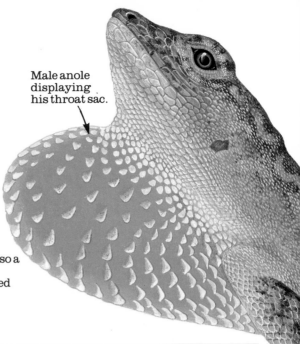

Male anole displaying his throat sac.

The display of the throat is also a sign of courtship to a female anole. The sac is usually folded against the anole's throat otherwise it would be easily spotted by hawks and other predators.

Thorny devil

The Moloch is a very prickly mouthful for a predator. Its body is covered with a mass of spikes as sharp as thorns. Apart from protecting this 15cm lizard, the spikes are very useful in the hot, dry desert as they collect water. Dew condenses on them and runs along tiny grooves in the Moloch's skin and into its mouth. This enables it to live for months without drinking.

Australian Moloch

Although it looks so fierce, the Moloch is quite harmless and eats only ants. It sits by an ant trail, flicking out its tongue and picking up 20 or 30 in a minute. One meal can consist of up to 1,500 ants which it crushes with its cheek teeth.

Rattle alarm ▶

The Rattlesnake warns intruders by sounding its alarm rattle. This gives an approaching animal time to escape and also saves the snake from being stepped on by large, hoofed animals. The rattle is made of loosely linked scaley sections which are the remains of the tail each time the snake sheds its skin. To sound the alarm, the snake vibrates its tail about 50 times a minute and the noise can be heard up to 30 metres away.

The snake sheds its skin three or four times a year, adding a new section to its tail each time. But the rattle cannot be used to tell the snake's age because the older ones start to wear off when there are about eight.

Rattle

Timber Rattlesnake of North America

Courtship

During the mating season, many male reptiles try to attract females with impressive displays. They also fight other males for mates and for territory.

Monitor wrestlers ▶

Male Monitor Lizards wrestle at the beginning of the mating season for female lizards. Surprisingly, neither male is hurt in these fights, although they are armed with sharp teeth and claws and strong tails. It seems that the wrestling is more a trial of strength than an attempt to kill each other — each lizard tries to push the other to the ground, and the first one to succeed wins the female.

The Two-Banded Monitor grows up to 3m long and is one of the largest lizards in the world. The gentlemanly mock battles only occur in the mating season. The Monitors do have very fierce fights over food which often result in bad injuries.

Two-Banded Monitor Lizard

Battering ram

The courtship of Greek Tortoises takes place in warm weather when they are able to move fairly quickly — up to 4.5km per hour, which is about the same speed as a man walking. The male chases his chosen female, and when he catches her he starts to butt her from behind, using his head like a battering ram. At the same time he bites her back legs quite fiercely. This onslaught makes the female draw her head and legs into the shell, and mating then takes place.

If the male cannot find a female during the breeding season, he has been known to butt anything in sight, from flower pots to people.

The male hisses while butting the female

Greek Tortoises – about 30cm long

TRUE or FALSE?

Boas tickle their mates

Cheek caressing ▶

In spring and early summer, the Painted Turtle male seeks out females and makes an attempt to court any one he comes across. He swims quickly after the female, overtakes, and turns to face her head on. She continues to swim on so the male is pushed backwards. In this face to face position, the male gently strokes the female's cheeks with his long foreclaws. If the female is receptive, she sinks to the bottom of the pond and allows the male to mate with her.

Common Night Adders of Africa grow 70-90cm long.

The female lays between 12 and 24 eggs which take up to 4 months to hatch.

◀ A love dance

Early in spring, Night Adders dance together as a prelude to mating. The male approaches the female from behind and rubs his chin and throat over her tail. He slowly jerks forward, moving himself along her body. After a while, the female slows down and throws her body in loops with the male following every move. He then wraps his tail around her body and twists, ready to mate.

Splashing out

Before courting starts, the male Nile Crocodile fights with other males to establish a breeding territory on the river bank. The male then patrols the patch of water close to the beach, bellowing at any rival male and fighting off intruders. When a female approaches, he gives off a strong smell of musk and roars. He claps his jaws and lashes his tail, sending clouds of spray all around. He swims in smaller and smaller circles round the female until he is close enough for them to mate.

The female choses a male with a territory which has good sunbathing and nest sites on the bank. She calls him with deep, husky noises.

Male Nile Crocodile

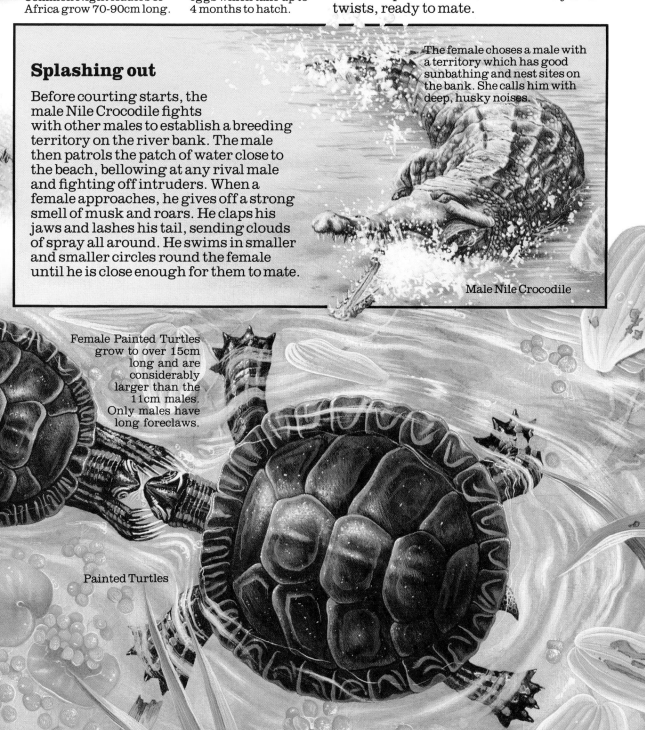

Female Painted Turtles grow to over 15cm long and are considerably larger than the 11cm males. Only males have long foreclaws.

Painted Turtles

Eggs and nurseries

Most reptiles lay eggs, although a few species do give birth to live young. All the ones that hatch from eggs have a special "tool" for breaking out of their shells; snakes and lizards have a sharp egg tooth, while tortoises and crocodiles have a horny knob on the end of their snouts.

Green Turtle hatchlings – they grow up to about 1½m.

Green Tree Python of New Guinea

The baby Pythons are born yellow or red and change to the rich green colour of the adult snakes when they are about 1m long. Adults grow up to about 2m.

Body warmers

Three to four months after mating, the female python lays up to 100 eggs. She gathers the eggs into a pile and coils her body around them for about three months until they hatch. By a special kind of shivering, the mother python can raise her body temperature by about 8°C while she incubates the eggs – an unusual ability in "cold-blooded" animals. She only leaves her eggs for occasional visits to the water and for rare meals.

Caring crocodiles ▶

Each year, the female Nile Crocodile lays up to 40 eggs in a nest dug in the sand above the waterline on the riverbank. She builds the nest in a shady place, about 20-30cm deep, so that the eggs keep at an even temperature – not varying more than 3°C. She covers the eggs with sand and both parents guard them during the 90 days incubation. Predators, such as the Nile Monitor, have a taste for crocodile eggs.

When it is ready to hatch, the young crocodile makes loud piping calls. Its mother scrapes away the sand covering the eggs, gently picks up each baby with her teeth, and carries them in a special pouch at the bottom of her mouth to a "nursery" pool area off the river. The young crocodiles follow their mother about like ducklings and crawl over her face and back.

The young crocodile stays in the "nursery" for about two months, guarded by its parents.

The first few steps of the Turtle's life are its most dangerous – it has to find its way to the sea past hungry crabs and Frigate Birds. The Turtles have more chance of reaching the sea if they make the dash together. Somehow the young Turtles know which direction to go when they leave their nests. They may follow the sound of the waves or head for the brighter light which is reflected off the sea.

Obstacle course ▲

The female Green Turtle lays her eggs in the sand dunes on the beaches of Ascension Island where they are incubated by the heat of the sun. She digs a nest with her hind flippers and, after laying about 100 eggs, covers them with sand and lumbers back to the sea. The male Turtle waits for her offshore, and they mate again and produce two or three more batches of eggs in the mating year. They usually return to the breeding grounds only once every three years.

On a limb

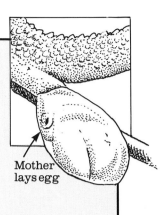

Mother lays egg

Most chameleons bury their parchment-like eggs underground and the babies then hatch about eight months later. The Dwarf Chameleon's eggs develop inside the mother's body and she gives birth to about 16 eggs which hatch almost immediately. The mother places each sticky egg carefully on a twig or leaf as they are laid. The young Chameleon then wriggles and twists its way out of the soft egg shell.

Egg sticks to twig

Chameleon twists out of the egg

The baby Dwarf Chameleon is only 3-4cm long, but it starts to hunt for insects within a few hours of being born. Adults grow up to 20cm.

The Nile Crocodile grows over 6m long.

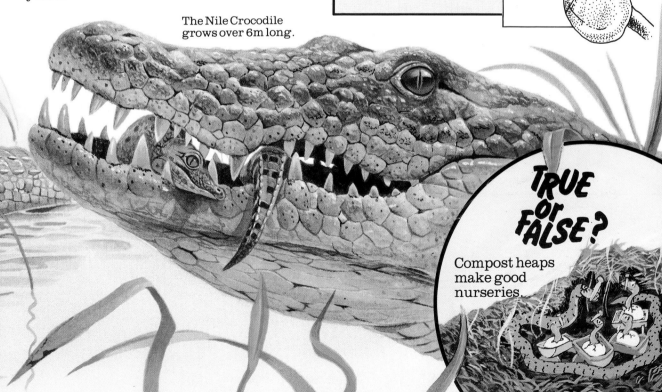

TRUE or FALSE?

Compost heaps make good nurseries.

On the move

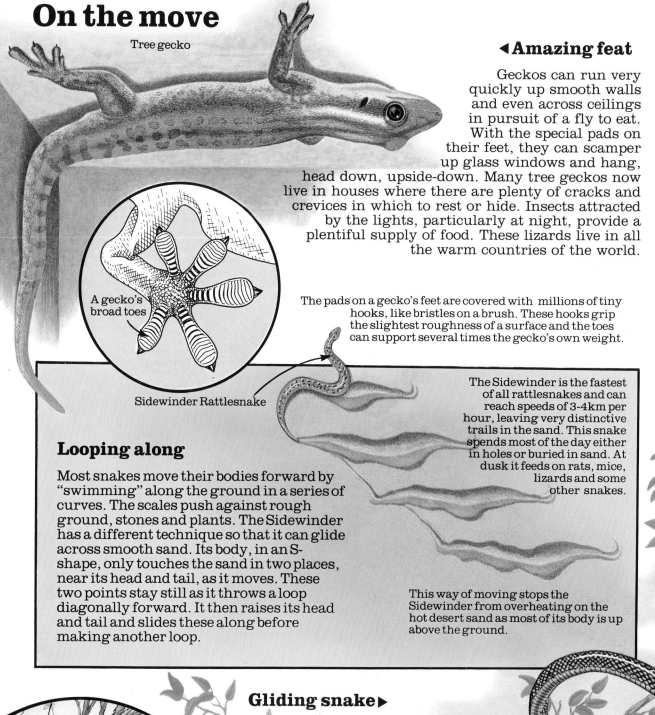

Tree gecko

A gecko's broad toes

Sidewinder Rattlesnake

◀ Amazing feat

Geckos can run very quickly up smooth walls and even across ceilings in pursuit of a fly to eat. With the special pads on their feet, they can scamper up glass windows and hang, head down, upside-down. Many tree geckos now live in houses where there are plenty of cracks and crevices in which to rest or hide. Insects attracted by the lights, particularly at night, provide a plentiful supply of food. These lizards live in all the warm countries of the world.

The pads on a gecko's feet are covered with millions of tiny hooks, like bristles on a brush. These hooks grip the slightest roughness of a surface and the toes can support several times the gecko's own weight.

Looping along

Most snakes move their bodies forward by "swimming" along the ground in a series of curves. The scales push against rough ground, stones and plants. The Sidewinder has a different technique so that it can glide across smooth sand. Its body, in an S-shape, only touches the sand in two places, near its head and tail, as it moves. These two points stay still as it throws a loop diagonally forward. It then raises its head and tail and slides these along before making another loop.

The Sidewinder is the fastest of all rattlesnakes and can reach speeds of 3-4km per hour, leaving very distinctive trails in the sand. This snake spends most of the day either in holes or buried in sand. At dusk it feeds on rats, mice, lizards and some other snakes.

This way of moving stops the Sidewinder from overheating on the hot desert sand as most of its body is up above the ground.

TRUE or FALSE?

Crocodiles climb trees.

Gliding snake ▶

The Paradise Snake can glide up to 35m from one tree to another. It launches itself from a branch, keeping its body in a S-shape and uses its tail like a rudder. By hollowing its body, it traps a cushion of air underneath which acts as a parachute and slows down its fall on to a lower branch.

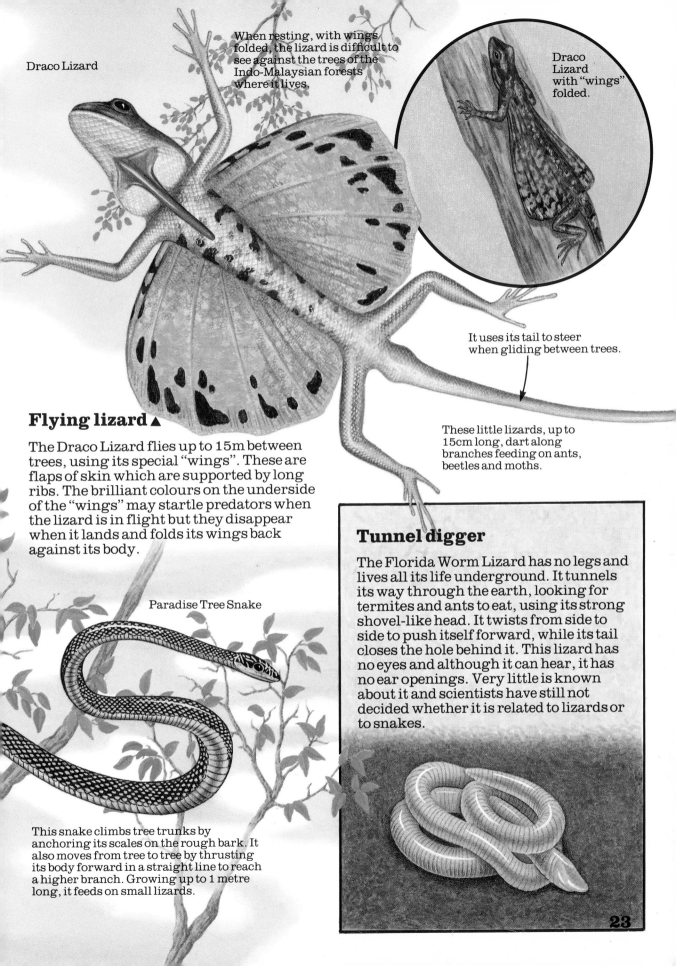

Draco Lizard

When resting, with wings folded, the lizard is difficult to see against the trees of the Indo-Malaysian forests where it lives.

Draco Lizard with "wings" folded.

It uses its tail to steer when gliding between trees.

Flying lizard ▲

The Draco Lizard flies up to 15m between trees, using its special "wings". These are flaps of skin which are supported by long ribs. The brilliant colours on the underside of the "wings" may startle predators when the lizard is in flight but they disappear when it lands and folds its wings back against its body.

These little lizards, up to 15cm long, dart along branches feeding on ants, beetles and moths.

Paradise Tree Snake

Tunnel digger

The Florida Worm Lizard has no legs and lives all its life underground. It tunnels its way through the earth, looking for termites and ants to eat, using its strong shovel-like head. It twists from side to side to push itself forward, while its tail closes the hole behind it. This lizard has no eyes and although it can hear, it has no ear openings. Very little is known about it and scientists have still not decided whether it is related to lizards or to snakes.

This snake climbs tree trunks by anchoring its scales on the rough bark. It also moves from tree to tree by thrusting its body forward in a straight line to reach a higher branch. Growing up to 1 metre long, it feeds on small lizards.

Taking to the water

Walking on the water ▶

The Basilisk Lizard escapes from its enemies by dropping on to the water from river-side trees or bushes. It then runs, at speeds up to 12kph, across the top of the water. It moves so fast on the long, fringed toes on its back legs that it does not have time to sink. If it does slow down, the lizard breaks through the surface of the water and swims, partly submerged, for the rest of its journey.

The Basilisk Lizard is called the Jésus Christo lizard in South America because it runs on water.

The Basilisk is named after the crested lizard which, according to the legend, hatched from an egg laid by a cockerel and could kill anything with just one glance. This iguanid lizard, which grows up to 60cm long, is quite harmless and feeds on plants and insects in tropical America.

The Anaconda can swim fast and often feeds on fish, turtles and even caimans.

◀ A swimming serpent

The Anaconda spends most of its day lying in the sluggish rivers or swamps of tropical South America, or sunbathing on low trees. At dusk it waits for its prey, usually birds and small mammals, to come down to the water to drink. Then it grabs its victim in its mouth and quickly loops its body round it. The snake slowly tightens its coils until its prey can no longer breathe and dies of suffocation, or drags it into the water to drown before eating it.

The snake eats its prey whole. A 7m Anaconda was reported to have swallowed a 2m caiman – a meal which would have lasted the snake for several weeks.

Submarine reptiles ▶

The Hawksbill Turtle, which lives in tropical seas around the world, has a light-weight shell and paddle-like legs. It uses its front legs to swim slowly through the water and its back legs to steer, like a rudder. The female Hawksbill crawls clumsily on land when she comes out to lay her eggs while the male rarely leaves the water.

Stone ballast ▼

The Gharial is a long, slender-snouted crocodile which lives in Indian rivers. It spends much of its time lying in the water with only its eyes and nostrils above the surface. Like all crocodiles, the Gharial swallows stones to help it stay under the water. Without this extra weight, young crocodiles become top heavy and would tip over. The Gharial can stay under the water for over an hour. It has special flaps which cover its nostrils and a valve which shuts off its windpipe so it can open its mouth to catch fish without swallowing lots of water.

TRUE or FALSE?

Crocodiles cry when eating their victims.

The lump on the end of some adults' snouts is a mystery. It may increase the noise of the mating call but no one really knows.

The Gharial's snout has over 100 sharp, even, teeth which it uses to catch fish.

The Hawksbill has always been hunted for its shell. Although plastics have largely replaced tortoise-shell, this turtle is still in danger of extinction.

The turtle eats water plants, sea urchins, fish and crabs. Its flesh is sometimes poisonous to human beings, perhaps because it also eats stinging jelly fish and Portuguese men-of-war.

Underwater grazing grounds

The Marine Iguana of the Galapagos Islands is the only lizard which is at home in the sea. There is little food on the barren volcanic shores and the lizard goes to sea for its meals of seaweed. When the tide goes out, exposing the reefs and algae-covered rocks, it plunges into the cool water. Clinging to the rocks with its sharp claws, it tears off the seaweed with its mouth. Some iguanas may swim out beyond the surf and dive down 5m to feed on the seabed, each dive lasting about 15 minutes.

Before diving into the cool sea, iguanas warm themselves in the sun. To avoid over-heating, they hold their bodies off the hot rocks or face the sun, so their heads provide shade for their bodies.

Marine Iguanas on Hood Island.

A place to live

Bird perch▼

Many snakes spend their lives in trees. The African Vine Snake lies along the branch of a tree with the front part of its 1.5m body held out stiffly in space. It stays motionless for hours, its long, slender body looking like a small branch to an unwary bird. It can move very fast through the trees, as well as on the ground, looking for meals of small birds and lizards.

Ruby-Topaz Hummingbird

The tiny Ruby-Topaz Hummingbird hovers near the snake, its wings beating 50-80 times a second.

The Vine Snake keeps its tongue quite still, instead of flicking it in and out like most snakes. It is thought that it may use its tongue as a bait to attract its prey.

African Vine Snake

At home in the sea

The Olive Sea Snake spends its life in warm, tropical Asian seas. Here it eats, breeds and produces live young, never leaving the water to go ashore. The snake's body is flat and its tail acts like an oar, driving it through the water. The snake breathes air and with special lungs, almost the length of its body, it can stay underwater for up to two hours. Flaps cover its nostrils when it is submerged. It can also "breathe" in air from the sea through its skin in much the same way as a fish "breathes" through its gills.

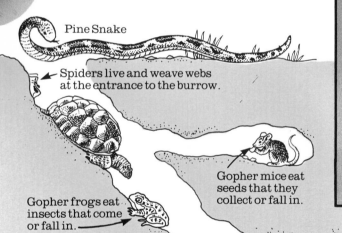

Pine Snake

Spiders live and weave webs at the entrance to the burrow.

Gopher mice eat seeds that they collect or fall in.

Gopher frogs eat insects that come or fall in.

Beetles feed on the tortoise's dung.

Cave crickets feed on beetle dung.

Shared shelter▲

The Gopher Tortoise digs its own home, a long, cool tunnel, amongst the sand hills of southern parts of the United States. Here it can escape during the day from the heat of the sun and it shares the burrow with several other animals. They all live together quite happily, each with its own place and habits. The tortoise can defend its home against unwelcome visitors, such as a Pine Snake, by blocking the entrance with its shell.

TRUE or FALSE?

Alligators live in sewers

Home of many lizards ▶

Most species of anoles live in trees, clinging to the branches with their long toes. They are found only in the Americas and particularly in the West Indies. In Cuba several kinds of these lizards live together in the same group of trees.

The 45cm Giant Anole lives in the tree tops where it hunts for frogs and young birds. A medium anole, 16cm long, lives on the tree trunks, while a third, slender anole, less than 13cm long, makes its home on the ground at the bottom of the trees.

Giant Anole

Huge numbers of snakes have been seen on the surface of the sea. There is one report of a belt of snakes in the Malacca Strait which was 3m wide and 96km long. No one knows why they mass together like this but it may happen during their mating season.

Females of all kinds of anole bury their eggs in shallow holes in the ground at the base of the trees. The eggs hatch in about six weeks.

The snake's body is pale underneath. This makes it difficult for fish, on which it feeds, to see it from below against the light of the sky.

Day and night shifts ▼

The Tuatara of New Zealand is the only survivor of a group of reptiles that became extinct millions of years ago. It usually lives in a burrow made by sea-birds such as petrels. Sleeping during the day, it comes out to feed at night on spiders, crickets and beetles. The petrel spends its day at sea and returns to the burrow at night.

Petrel

The Tuatara's name means "spine bearer" in Maori language. It gets this name from the crest running along its back.

On the top of the Tuatara's head is an extra eye, covered by skin – no one knows what this is for.

No one knows why the Petrel allows the Tuatara to be its "house guest" as their relationship is not always friendly. The Tuatara will sometimes eat the bird's eggs, the young chicks and even the adult bird. the Petrel occasionally takes its revenge by eating baby Tuataras.

Tuatara

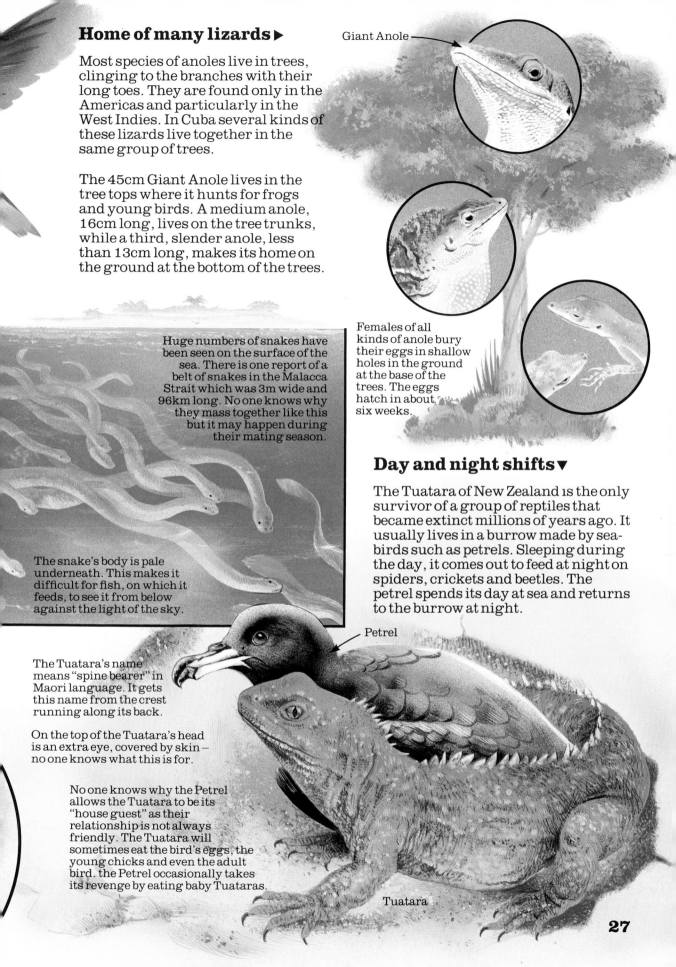

Curious events

Living toothbrush ▶

During the heat of the day, the crocodile lies on a muddy bank with its mouth wide open. Water evaporates from its mouth, cooling it down, rather like a dog panting when hot. Plovers land on its jaw to peck food from its teeth. They seem to be in no danger. This may be because they clean the crocodile's teeth, which it cannot do itself as its tongue is not moveable. The birds may also remove leeches and other irritating insects.

No one knows why the inside of its mouth is such a brilliant colour, but the crocodile may use it as a shock tactic – suddenly opening its mouth and freezing its prey with terror.

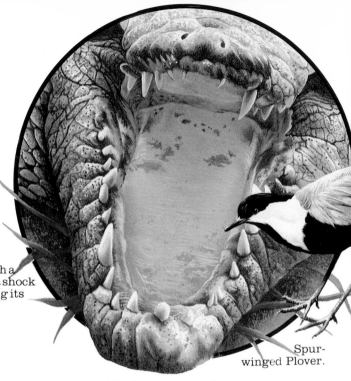

Spur-winged Plover.

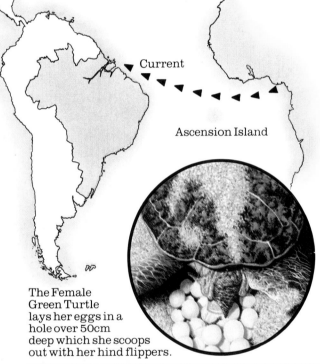

Current

Ascension Island

The Female Green Turtle lays her eggs in a hole over 50cm deep which she scoops out with her hind flippers.

◀ Long distance swimmers

Every three years, groups of Green Turtles gather together and swim 2,000km from their grazing grounds off the coast of Brazil to lay their eggs on Ascension Island. No one knows how the Turtles manage to find the small 13km by 9km island in the middle of the Atlantic. There is an ocean current running at just under 2km per hour from the African coast, past Ascension Island, to Brazil. To return to their grazing grounds the Turtles just have to drift with this. But as their swimming speed is only 2km per hour, they cannot go against the current on the outward journey and must find another route. Scientists think that they either follow smells given off by different parts of the sea, or navigate by means of the sun and stars. The round trip takes about three years.

Snake eats snake ▶

When a Rattlesnake comes across a King Snake it acts in a very unusual way. Instead of preparing to strike with its poison-injecting fangs, the rattler keeps its head as far as possible from the King Snake and uses the middle of its body to try to beat it off. The King Snake, not put off, grasps the rattler's neck in its teeth, wraps its body round the rattler and chokes it to death. The non-poisonous King Snake is successful in these battles because it is immune to the rattler's, usually lethal, poison.

The King Snake also attacks and eats other King Snakes.

A two-headed serpent ▶

Occasionally freak two-headed snakes are born. A two-headed King Snake which lived in San Diego Zoo was always in danger because of the King Snake's habit of eating other snakes. One night one of the heads tried to swallow the other. The attacked head was rescued in the morning by a keeper, but it later tried to take its revenge on the first head and this attack killed both heads and their one body.

The two-headed snake of San Diego Zoo also had two lungs, instead of one, and two hearts.

Rafts ▼

Scientists think that the reptiles on the Galapagos Islands reached there by means of natural rafts from the coast of Equador, 800-900km away. A tortoise, for example, would climb on to a piece of drift wood to rest, which then drifted out to sea.

Mammals are less able than reptiles to cope with the lack of food and water on rafts, and the Rice Rats are the only native land mammals which exist on the Galapagos Islands.

Stowaways ▶

Geckos living in ports quite often find their way on to ships while searching for insect meals. They have travelled to remote parts of the world on these ships as "stowaways" – the Turkish Gecko has migrated to most of the world's main tropical areas in this way.

California King Snake.

It swallows the Rattlesnake by "walking" its mouth and body over the dead snake.

TRUE or FALSE?

Snakes can jump a metre high.

Record breakers

The biggest meal

The biggest meal recorded was an Impala weighing nearly 60kg found in the stomach of a 4.87m African Rock Python.

The most deaths

In India, Indian Cobras kill about 7,500 people per year which is about 25% of all the snake bite deaths in India.

Smallest snakes

Thread Snakes are only 1 to 1.3cm long and are so thin they could glide through the hole left in a normal pencil if the lead was removed.

Fastest snake

The Black Mamba can reach speeds of 25km per hour in short bursts. It races along with its head and the front of its body raised, mouth open and tongue flicking.

Tiny but loud

The Least Geckos are the smallest reptiles at only 2½cm long. Some of these tiny lizards sing in loud chirrups, which can be heard up to 10km away and attract mates.

The largest reptile

Salt-water Crocodiles are today's largest reptiles. They grow to an average of 4½m long, although there have been reports of larger beasts. A 8m Crocodile was killed in 1954 which was over 1.5m tall at the shoulder and would have weighed nearly 2 tons.

The longest starvation

The Okinawa Habu Snake of the West Pacific can survive for more than 3 years without food.

The longest fangs

The highly venomous Gaboon Viper of Tropical Africa has the longest fangs of any snake. One 1.2m snake had fangs nearly 3cm long. It will only bite if really provoked.

Fastest swimming snake

The Yellow-bellied Sea Snake of the Indo-Pacific region can swim at the rate of 1m per second. Sea Snakes can also dive 100m deep and stay under water for up to 5 hours.

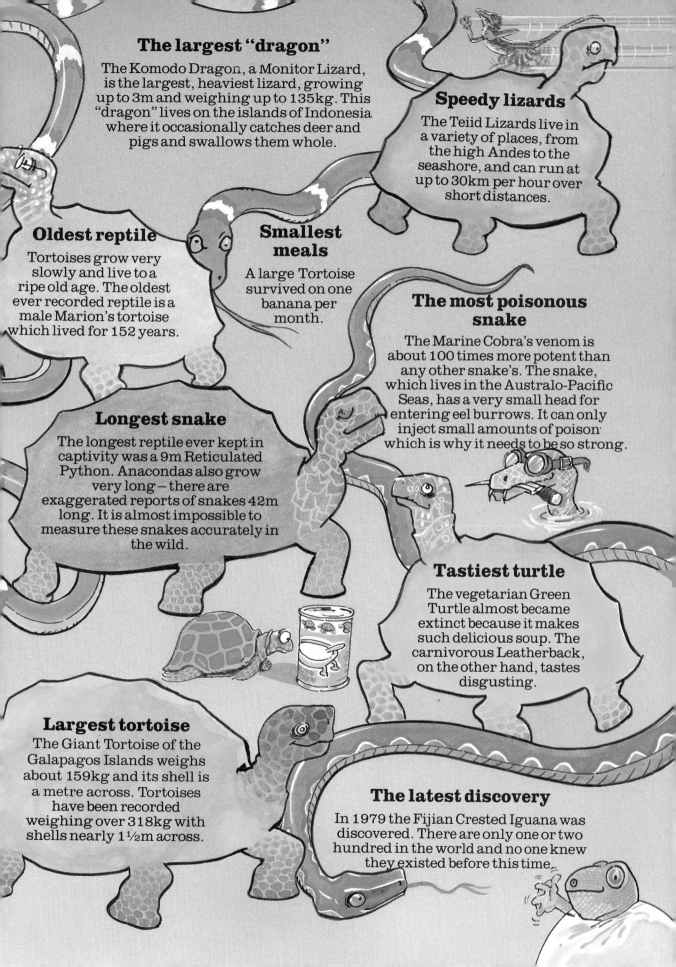

The largest "dragon"

The Komodo Dragon, a Monitor Lizard, is the largest, heaviest lizard, growing up to 3m and weighing up to 135kg. This "dragon" lives on the islands of Indonesia where it occasionally catches deer and pigs and swallows them whole.

Speedy lizards

The Teiid Lizards live in a variety of places, from the high Andes to the seashore, and can run at up to 30km per hour over short distances.

Oldest reptile

Tortoises grow very slowly and live to a ripe old age. The oldest ever recorded reptile is a male Marion's tortoise which lived for 152 years.

Smallest meals

A large Tortoise survived on one banana per month.

The most poisonous snake

The Marine Cobra's venom is about 100 times more potent than any other snake's. The snake, which lives in the Australo-Pacific Seas, has a very small head for entering eel burrows. It can only inject small amounts of poison which is why it needs to be so strong.

Longest snake

The longest reptile ever kept in captivity was a 9m Reticulated Python. Anacondas also grow very long – there are exaggerated reports of snakes 42m long. It is almost impossible to measure these snakes accurately in the wild.

Tastiest turtle

The vegetarian Green Turtle almost became extinct because it makes such delicious soup. The carnivorous Leatherback, on the other hand, tastes disgusting.

Largest tortoise

The Giant Tortoise of the Galapagos Islands weighs about 159kg and its shell is a metre across. Tortoises have been recorded weighing over 318kg with shells nearly 1½m across.

The latest discovery

In 1979 the Fijian Crested Iguana was discovered. There are only one or two hundred in the world and no one knew they existed before this time.

Were they true or false?

page 5 Skinks have antifreeze in their blood.
TRUE. The Water Skink of the Eastern Australian mountains emerges from its hybernation when there is still snow on the ground. Antifreeze in its blood keeps it active even when its body temperature is $-2°C$.

page 7 Cobras dance to the music of the snake charmer's pipe.
FALSE. The Cobra cannot hear the music. When its basket is opened, it rises in defence and then follows the movement of the pipe, ready to attack.

page 11 Snakes have been used as weapons of war.
TRUE. It is said that Hannibal had jars of live poisonous snakes thrown into his enemy's ships – a tactic which resulted in victory.

page 13 Chameleons turn black with rage.
PARTLY TRUE. Using its ability to change colour, the Chameleon may turn nearly black when faced by an enemy.

page 15 Crocodiles pretend to be logs to escape from enemies.
FALSE. The crocodile does look like a log but this is to stalk its prey.

page 18 Boas tickle their mates.
TRUE. Boas have spurs which are all that remain of back legs. The male uses his to scratch and tickle the female during courtship.

page 21 Compost heaps make good nurseries.
TRUE. Grass Snakes seek warm, moist places to lay their eggs – a compost heap is ideal.

page 22 Crocodiles climb trees.
TRUE. Young crocodiles are good climbers and often rest on branches near water.

page 25 Crocodiles cry when eating their victims.
FALSE. Saltwater Crocodiles are often seen to cry on land, but this is to rid themselves of excess salt, not remorse.

page 26 Alligators live in sewers.
PARTLY TRUE. There are reports of alligators in the sewers beneath Manhatten Island, U.S.A. These were probably pets, released into drains when their owners became bored with them.

page 29 Snakes can jump a meter high.
TRUE. A Viper of Central America can leap up to 1m to strike at its prey.

Index

Adder
  Dwarf Puff, 4
  Night, 19
Alligator, 5
Anaconda, 24, 31
Anole, 17, 27
  Giant, 27

Badger, 15
Beetle, 26
Birds
  Petrel, 27
  Ruby-Topaz Hummingbird, 26
  Spur-winged Plover, 28
Boa Constrictor, 18
  Anaconda, 24
  Brazilian Rainbow Boa, 8-9
  Rubber, 15
Boomslang, 11

Caiman, 24
Chameleon, 11, 13, 21
  African, 6
  Common African, 6
  Dwarf, 21
  Graceful, 8
  Jackson's, 2
Cobra, 7
  Indian, 30
  King, 10-11
  Marine, 31
  Spitting, 10
Copperhead

American, 6-7
Cricket, Cave, 26
Crocodile, 3, 5, 14-15, 22, 25, 28
  Nile, 19, 20-21
  Saltwater, 30

Dragon
  Bearded, 12
  Komodo, 31

Fer-de-Lance, 11
Frog, Gopher, 26

Galapagos Islands, 25, 29, 31
Gecko
  Leaf-tailed, 16
  Least, 30
  Ocellated, 3
  Tokay, 6
  Tree, 22
  Turkish, 29
Gharial, 25
Gila Monster, 10

Horned Toad, 14-15
Hummingbird, Ruby-Topaz, 26

Iguana
  Common, 3
  Fijian Crested, 31
  Marine, 25

Jacobson's organ, 7

King Snake, 29
  Californian, 28-29
  Milk Snake, 14

Lizard
  Armadillo, 13
  Basilisk, 24-25
  Bearded, 12
  Florida Worm, 23
  Frilled, 12, 16
  Fringe-toed, 4
  Gecko, 23
  Gila Monster, 10
  Horned Toad, 14-15
  Jewelled, 5
  Mexican Beaded, 10
  Moloch, 16-17
  Shingleback, 4
  Teiid, 31

Mamba, Black, 30
Mice, Gopher, 26
Moloch, 16-17
Mongoose, 10
Monitor Lizard, 2-3
  Komodo Dragon, 31
  Nile, 21
  Two-Banded, 18

Petrel, 27
Plover, Spur-winged, 28
Python, 9
  African Rock, 30
  Green Tree, 20
  Reticulated, 31

Royal Ball, 3

Rat
  Kangaroo, 7
  Rice, 29
Rattlesnake, 14, 28-29
  Sidewinder, 22
  Timber, 17

Scales, 5
Skink, 5
  Sudanese, 15
  Water, 32
Snake, 11, 22, 29
  African Egg-eating, 9
  African Vine, 26
  American Copperhead, 6-7
  American Hognosed, 14
  Australian Blind, 9
  Boomslang, 11
  Coral, 14
  European Rat, 6
  Fer-de-Lance, 11
  Grass, 32
  Milk, 14
  Okinawa Habu, 30
  Olive Sea, 26-27
  Paradise Tree, 22-23
  Pine, 26
  Rattlesnake, 14, 17, 22, 28-29
  Thread, 30

Two-headed, 29
  Yellow Bellied Sea, 30
Spider, 23
Stinkpot Turtle, 12

Termites, Compass, 9
Tortoise, 29, 31
  Giant Galapagos, 2, 31
  Gopher, 26
  Greek, 18
  Marion's, 31
  Radiated, 13
Tortoise-shell, 25
Tuatara, 5, 27
Turtle
  Alligator Snapping, 8
  Big-headed, 12
  Green, 20-21, 28, 31
  Hawksbill, 24-25
  Leatherback, 31
  Matamata, 8
  Painted, 18-19
  Red Bellied, 2
  Snake-necked, 12
  Stinkpot, 12

Viper, 10
  American Copperhead, 6-7
  Gaboon, 30
  Pit, 2-3

Worm Lizard, 23